P9-CQQ-006

SEX, LOVE, AND OTHER PROBLEMS

SEX, LOVE, AND OTHER PROBLEMS

CARTOONS BY DAVID SIPRESS

A PLUME BOOK

For Ginny

PLUME
Published by the Penguin Group
Penguin Books USA Inc., 375 Hudson Street, New York, New York 10014, U.S.A.
Penguin Books Ltd, 27 Wrights Lane, London W8 5TZ, England
Penguin Books Australia Ltd, Ringwood, Victoria, Australia
Penguin Books Canada Ltd, 2801 John Street, Markham, Ontario, Canada L3R 1B4
Penguin Books (N.Z.) Ltd, 182-190 Wairau Road, Auckland 10, New Zealand

Penguin Books Ltd, Registered Offices: Harmondsworth, Middlesex, England

First published by Plume, an imprint of New American Library,
a division of Penguin Books USA Inc.

First Printing, May, 1991
10 9 8 7 6 5 4 3 2 1

Copyright © David Sipress, 1991
All rights reserved

Some of the cartoons in this book appeared previously in *The Boston Phoenix,*
New Woman, and *Woman.*

 REGISTERED TRADEMARK—MARCA REGISTRADA

LIBRARY OF CONGRESS CATALOGING-IN-PUBLICATION DATA:

Sipress, David.
    Sex, love, and other problems / by David Sipress.
        p.   cm.
    ISBN 0-452-26614-9 : $5.95
        1. Sex—Humor.   2. Love—Humor.   I. Title.
    PN6231.S54S49   1991
    741.5'973—dc20

90-24606
CIP

Printed in the United States of America

Without limiting the rights under copyright reserved above, no part of this publication
may be reproduced, stored in or introduced into a retrieval system, or transmitted, in any
form, or by any means (electronic, mechanical, photocopying, recording, or otherwise),
without the prior written permission of both the copyright owner and the above publisher of
this book.

BOOKS ARE AVAILABLE AT QUANTITY DISCOUNTS WHEN USED TO PROMOTE PRODUCTS OR SERVICES.
FOR INFORMATION PLEASE WRITE TO PREMIUM MARKETING DIVISION, PENGUIN BOOKS USA INC.,
375 HUDSON STREET, NEW YORK, NEW YORK 10014.

Don't ever give up, Marjorie, I never thought I'd meet anyone either.

I'm supposed to meet a SWF, Gemini, 30-35, who loves skiing, hiking, dancing, and just sitting around watching old movies.

Normally I don't go out on blind dates, but when my sister said you also had a philodendron growing out of the top of your head, I thought, "What the hell..."
SIPRESS

Be positive, Cheryl! Keep telling yourself,
"Looks don't matter, looks don't matter."

In preparation for our date I've written my auto-
biography to help you get to know me a
little better.

You know, I don't usually go out with men like you,
but at this point I'll try _anything_.

Can I fax you sometime?

SIPRESS

How it came to be that Mark and Doris never got together.

SIPRESS

O.K., Class, we'll start with a five-minute warm-up, followed by ten minutes of low impact, twenty minutes of high impact, and then we'll all get down on the floor and have sex with the gentleman in the back row.

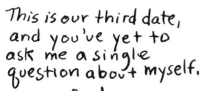

SIPRESS

I'd ask you in, Marshall, but I have to get up early, my roommate is asleep, I still have a little work to do, and I find you totally unattractive.

CONDOMS n' STUFF

SIPRESS

Can you recommend a pornographic film for two
people with advanced degrees in modern philosophy?

Lay a hand on her and I'll scratch your eyes out.

I'm sure many men are scared off by your wealth and success. I, on the other hand, would have the courage to be totally dependent on you.

There's a message from your lawyer, a message from your sister, and a mixed message from your boyfriend.

SIPRESS

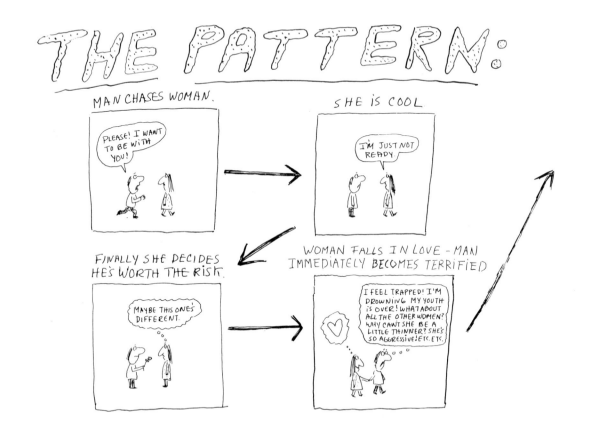

We're going to be covering each other's naked body with the ice cream, and then licking it off, so we'd prefer a flavor that doesn't have a lot of chips or nuts or other junk in it.

SIPRESS

Honey, have you seen my diaphragm?

SIPRESS

It's so nice to actually meet Larry's parents! I must say, you're not at all the way he described you.

I'm being evicted, you have an apartment.
It's perfect! Let's get married!

So do you, Ellen, and do you, Harold, accept and approve, for better and for worse, this prenuptial agreement?

DIALOGUE ABOUT THE RELATIONSHIP

O.K, Charlie, I'll accept that it's my fault that it's raining. But I also want full credit when the sun comes out!

SIPRESS

All right! I'll go with you to see a couples' therapist. Who knows? Maybe he can figure out what's wrong with you.
SIPRESS

Of course I want you to tell me how you feel about things, Carl. Don't hold back anything! But just remember, it'll be your fault if I get really upset.
SIPRESS

I just hope we can make the house payment! Then we've got to fix the car! When am I going to finish that report? I just know they're gonna fire me, then what'll we do?? I wonder if Billy is taking drugs. The kid's been acting so weird lately, I'm sure I've really screwed him up! God! I feel fat, I've got to lose some weight...
ZZZ
Honey, wake up! It's 3 A.M.
Hmm?
Would you mind taking over?
Oh sure, it's my turn anyway.
ZZZ
How in the world can we afford Billy's school? And how will we ever make the house payment? Boy! Have I been messing up at work! I hope I don't lose my job. Ouch! What was that? Oh great, I'm having a heart attack! Wow, we've got to get better insurance - what if something happened? And then there's taxes...
SIPRESS

I hope you won't take this as criticism, but you look awful tonight.

The most I really can do is describe the dishes to you. As for your need of help in making a decision, may I suggest the two of you consult a competent therapist.

My husband won't be joining us this evening.
He's undergoing extensive renovations.

SIPRESS

Honey, you seem preoccupied.

Let me introduce my husband and his own worst enemy.

Sweetheart, did I enjoy it the last time we had sex?

It has come to our attention that you've been thinking of other women while making love to your wife.

I need some space.

ABOUT THE AUTHOR

David Sipress is the author of *It's a Mom's Life, It's a Dad's Life,* and *The Secret Life of Dogs.* A cartoonist and sculptor, he currently resides in New York City. His work has appeared in *Spy, Harper's, New Woman, Family Circle, Psychology Today,* and *The Boston Phoenix.*